TRAIL QUEST

A guide to leisure trails around North West Water land

SUITABLE FOR ALL AGES AND ABILITIES

Written by
Gillian Rowan-Wilde

GILDERSLEVE
PUBLISHING LIMITED

DOING THE RIGHT THING

North West Water has a key role as a custodian of land in the north west of England working in partnership to protect and enhance our areas of natural beauty for the benefit of those who live, work and visit, as well as for future generations.

We provide water and wastewater services to seven million people in the north west of England and our role is to collect, clean and distribute vital water. The region's daily water comes from catchments where reservoirs and surrounding areas are managed and protected, to deliver quality drinking water.

A crucial aspect of our role is to balance the increasing demand for water with desire for conservation, access and recreation. We will continue to improve access for people who enjoy walking, fishing and observing wildlife, whilst preserving the quality of the water and recognising the needs of the environment.

We work in partnership with the British Trust for Conservation Volunteers, the County Wildlife Trusts, English Nature, Lake District and Peak District National Park Authorities, National Trust, Royal Society for the Protection of Birds and our farming tenants. We have a long term commitment to community partnerships and have recently celebrated twenty one years of working with British Trust for Conservation Volunteers - conserving and rebuilding footpaths, dry stone walls and planting trees together.

As part of our commitment to enhancing children's learning we have a network of Environmental Education Centres visited by more than 7,000 children each year who learn about the value of water in our lives.

As part of our commitment to allow access to our land to all, regardless of age or ability, we are delighted to work in partnership with Age Concern in the development of this book.

Proceeds from the sale of this book will go towards furthering the partnership for the benefit of Age Concern projects in the North West.

ACCESS FOR ALL

AGE *Concern*
IN THE
NORTH WEST

Age Concern organisations aim to promote the well-being of all older people and help make later life a fulfilling and enjoyable experience.

As caring organisations, Age Concern works in local communities to provide direct help and services for frail older people who need support and preventative services aimed at promoting the health and well-being of older people. A wide range of practical help and support and advisory services are offered to individual older people and their carers. Age Concern also runs a number of innovative leisure and social activities for people from their early 50's onwards.

Part of the role of Age Concern is to ensure that older people have access to the information and advice they need, when they need it. Age Concern's work with older people also forms the basis for a continuing programme of informing and educating policy and decision makers and representing and communicating the needs of older people to the public at large.

Age Concern is also continually searching for innovative and effective ways of meeting the needs of older people. This involves a continual review of practices and the growth of a positive and constructive attitude towards the design and delivery of services at every level.

Each Age Concern organisation seeks to foster a capacity to respond to the individual needs of older people, across all sectors, and to encourage joint action and joint decision making on priorities and action.

Age Concern organisations in the North West are delighted to work with North West Water in producing this book. We particularly hope that many older people will enjoy the trails. By purchasing the book you have helped to support Age Concern's work in the North West. We rely on local volunteers and local donations. If you would like more information on services or opportunities for older people, volunteering or more information about Age Concern's range of insurance products, please contact your local Age Concern organisation - you will find the telephone number in your telephone directory, or return the reply card at the back of this book.

Age Concern organisations are Registered Charities

INTRODUCTION

"I feel comfortable walking round the woods, shuffling through the leaves because I feel I'm inside of something - I've got roots"

John Hayes

Like John I feel the same about the north west - Having lived, for the last twenty five years in Rossendale which is situated on the edge of the Pennines. I have for relaxation and exercise escaped the pressures of business and wandered the cloughs and moors above industrial Lancashire - here I found a new world of grouse and heather, meandering streams and the ruins of a bygone era. A landscape of ever changing moods, often wet, the weather itself bringing its own particular beauty, clagg mists and a brisk breeze are common during the winter months. It was these elements that convinced our forefathers to build the reservoirs in and around these rain soaked hills. Some of these catchments were built to supply the canal system and others to supply drinking water for the rapidly expanding mill towns and cities in the north west.

North West Water is now the owner of the majority of these reservoirs and the land surrounding

them. In compiling this guide Gillian and myself have visited these sites and walked or cycled most of the trails in this book. During our journeying we were continually amazed at the amount of resource that North West Water has put into maintaining and improving the environment surrounding their properties.

The North West Water slogan ACCESS FOR ALL means just that. Whether you are a walker, cyclist, able or a person with a disability, young or old you will find a trail on their land to suit you. We hope you enjoy using this book as much as we have compiling it and wish you many happy hours exploring what is some of the most rewarding recreational countryside in the north west.

Peter

Peter Gildersleve

ACKNOWLEDGMENTS

1. Whilst we have made every effort to achieve accuracy in the preparation of material for this guide book, the author, publisher and copyright owners can take no responsibility for trespass, irresponsible riding, any loss or damage to persons or property suffered as a result of the route descriptions or advice in this book.

2. All rights reserved.
No part of this publication may be reproduced, stored in a retrieval system, or transmitted in any form or by any means, electronic, mechanical, photocopied, recording or otherwise, without the prior permission of the Publisher and the copyright holder.

3. All text copyright Gillian Rowan-Wilde.
The contents of this publication are believed correct at the time of printing. Nevertheless, the Publishers cannot accept responsibility for errors and omissions, or for changes in details given.

Wilde's Leisure Guides are a trade mark of Gildersleve Publishing Ltd.

© Copyright Gillian Rowan-Wilde
Published by
Gildersleve Publishing Ltd
Capricorn House, Blackburn Road
Rising Bridge, Lancashire BB5 2AA

ACKNOWLEDGMENTS
Mike Crabtree head of conservation access and recreation at North West Water, his Team Leaders and countyside rangers for their help in supplying information and checking maps. Helen and Tracy for their patience.

Maps compiled from information supplied by North West Water.

COUNTRYSIDE CODE

Wherever you go it makes sense to act responsibly and follow the practical guidelines which make up the Country Code.

- Enjoy the countryside and respect its life and work
- Guard against all risk of fire
- Fasten all gates
- Keep your dogs under close control
- Keep to public paths across farmland
- Use gates and stiles to cross fences, hedges and walls
- Leave livestock, crops and machinery alone
- Take your litter home
- Help to keep all water clean
- Protect wildlife, plants and trees
- Take special care on country roads
- Make no unnecessary noise

DOG CODE

Please keep your dogs under close control at all times or on the lead - this is particularly important in the Spring during lambing season (Please note there are no dogs allowed at Worthington Lakes).

TRAIL GRADING

EASY	No Hills
EASY, ADVENTUROUS	As above but with a hill - easily negotiable
MODERATE	Forest paths, Lakeside, Moorland. A hill, stream or rough ground - easily negotiable.
HARD	Fells or Forest with hills. Several hills with a degree of difficulty and ground may be undulating.
HARD, ADVENTUROUS	As above but with longer hills and steeper gradients.

HOW TO GET THE MOST OUT OF YOUR VISITS

This book has been designed to give the user a choice of various trails. Each location shows one or more of these icons which show the type of trails available

 WALKERS

 PEOPLE WITH DISABILITIES

 CYCLISTS

The trails indicated by a thick red line on the map indicates the easiest route, on some maps ② ③indicates a second or third choice, these are usually more strenuous.

Other trail choices can be self selected by using the marked footpaths, bridleways and roads. Specific routes for wheelchairs and cyclists are indicated with their own markings. Cycling red dots and wheelchairs green or black dots.

(Please note cyclists must only use indicated cycle routes, bridleways or roads)

CONTENTS

LEGEND

🎣	Fishing	🏰	Castle
≈	Water sports	🚶	Walking Route
🐴	Bridleway	🚲	Cycling Route
🧺	Picnic area	👫	Walkers
🌿	Nature reserve	⚒	Ruin
ℹ	Information centre	🅿	Parking
🏫	Education Centre	🚴	Cyclists
♿	Facilities for people with disabilities	🚩	Golf
👁	Viewpoint	▲	Mountain
⛰	Climbing	WC	Toilets
🌳	Forest or woodland	🚆	Railway Station
🏛	Historic building	⚷	RADAR Key
☁	Weather warning	👁	Tapping Rail

N.W.W. designated trail ——————

Trail for wheelchairs ••••/••••

Trail for the visually impaired ▪▬▪▬▪

Cycle trail •••••••••

Footpath - Public Right of Way ▬ ▬ ▬

Concessionary Footpath — — — —

Bridleway - Public Right of Way — - — - —

Concessionary Bridleway — •• — •• —

National Park Boundary

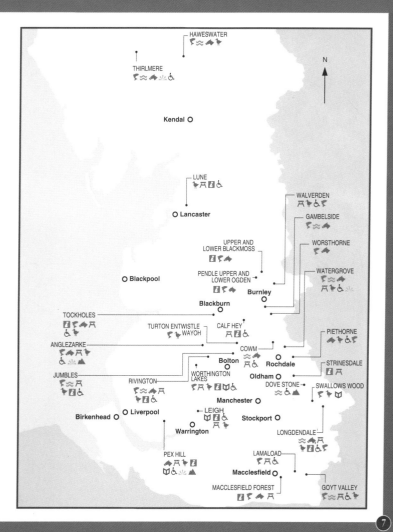

THE HAWESWATER ESTATE

START & FINISH
Car park at Mardale Head

MAP
O/S Outdoor Leisure No.5 (N.E. English Lakes)

SURFACE
Gravel/grass/ tarmac

ROUTE RATING
Bill Foster Memorial Trail - Easy
Route 2 Riggendale Horseshoe - Hard
Other routes - Medium Adventurous

PROVISION FOR PEOPLE WITH DISABILITIES
Not suitable for wheelchairs

The Haweswater Estate is situated in the eastern edge of the Lake District west of Shap and the M6 motorway, and east of the A592 Troutbeck to Patterdale road.

The late Bill Foster

Haweswater Lake is in a beautiful area surrounded by magnificently high hills with some tremendous walks.

Haweswater originally was a natural lake. After 1919, the volume of water was increased threefold due to the increasing demand for water. This completely submerged the hamlet of Mardale.

The dam was the first hollow buttress dam in the world completed in the 1930's.

The first route is along the Bill Foster Memorial Trail although easy, the ground does undulate and can be stoney.

Bill Foster, North West Water's Conservation, Access and Recreation Director, died in November 1994. He had made an immense contribution to the North West Water which he joined in 1975. Bill developed strong links with national parks, local authorities and conservation groups, many of which are now represented on the Company's Conservation, Access and Recreation Advisory Committee - the creation of which was one of his proudest achievements. In 1989 Bill played a key role in drafting the recreational Code of Practice which set national standards.

The second route 'Riggindale Horseshoe' is a great favourite because of the magnificent views of the surrounding hills and Martindale Forest. It is a steep climb up onto High Street via Riggindale Crag, but well worth the effort.

Looking over towards Harter Fell and High Street

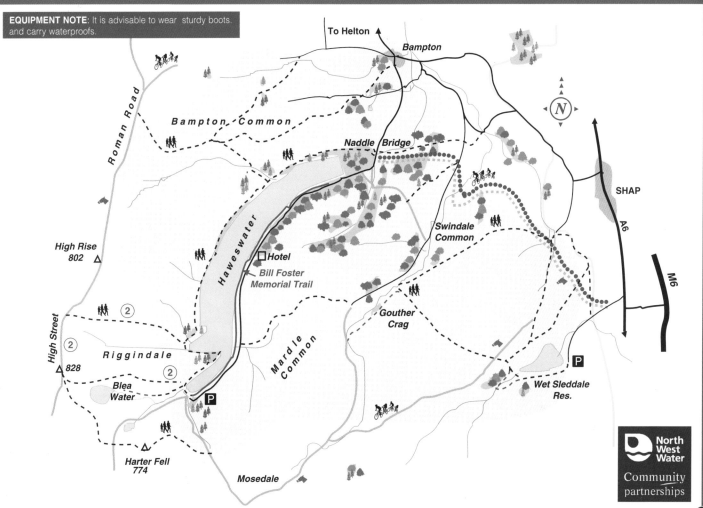

EQUIPMENT NOTE: It is advisable to wear sturdy boots. and carry waterproofs.

To Helton

Bampton

Roman Road

Bampton Common

Naddle Bridge

SHAP

A6

M6

High Rise
802

Swindale
Common

Haweswater

□ Hotel

Bill Foster
Memorial Trail

High Street

2

2

Riggindale

2

828

Blea
Water

Mardle
Common

Gouther
Crag

Wet Sleddale
Res.

P

P

Harter Fell
774

Mosedale

North West Water

Community partnerships

THIRLMERE ESTATE

START & FINISH
Car park beside The Swirls Forest Trail

MAP
O/S Outdoor Leisure 4 / 5
(Englsih lakes N.E./N.W.)

LENGTH (approx)
Trails of varying lengths

SURFACE
Gravel/grass /tarmaac

ROUTE RATING
Moderate Adventurous - Hard

PROVISION FOR PEOPLE WITH DISABILITIES
Wheelchair access at Swirls and Legburthwaite car park. Toilet facilities.

Helvellyn from the west side of Thirlmere.

The Thirlmere Estate is in the north central area of the Lake District, south of Keswick with the Helvellyn range of hills to the east and Grasmere to the south.

There are numerous varying levels of walks in this area. Walking around the lake is a wonderful experience looking across the water to the Helvellyn range of high mountains that separate Thirlmere from Ullswater.

The more adventurous and steep climb up onto the ridge to Dollywagon Pike and Helvellyn is one of those never-to-be forgotten experiences, the panoramic view of the Lake District from the top of this ridge are aweinspiring. The track up onto the ridge is by way of an old pack horse route and although well graded this old route is none the less a very steep climb.

Launchy Gill

It is well worth exploring the surrounding area of the reservoir, particularly Harrop Tarn and Raven Crag on the western shore, and on the eastern side, the waterfalls above the nature trail in Helvellyn Gill.

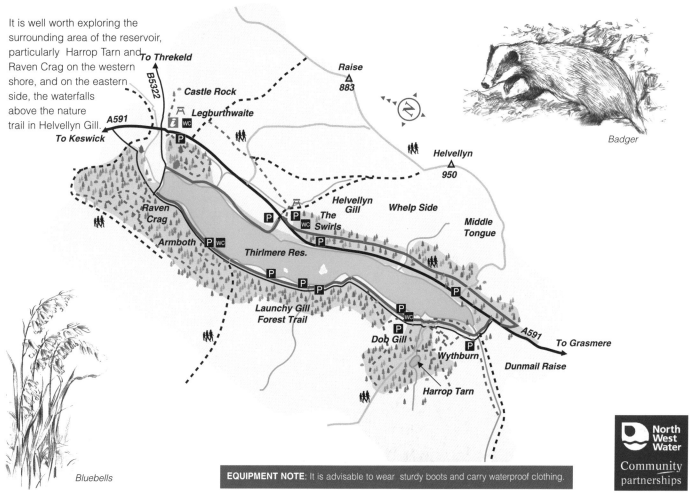

To Threkeld

B5322

Castle Rock

Legburthwaite

A591

To Keswick

Raven Crag

Armboth

Raise
△ 883

Helvellyn
△ 950

Helvellyn Gill

Whelp Side

The Swirls

Middle Tongue

Thirlmere Res.

Launchy Gill Forest Trail

Dob Gill

Wythburn

Harrop Tarn

A591

To Grasmere

Dunmail Raise

Badger

Bluebells

EQUIPMENT NOTE: It is advisable to wear sturdy boots and carry waterproof clothing.

WORTHINGTON LAKES

START & FINISH
Worthington Lakes Environmental
Education Centre Car Park

MAP
O/S Landranger 108 (Liverpool)
Explorer 19 (West Pennine Moors)

LENGTH (approx)
1 km (½ m) Circular Arley
Route 2 - 3½ km (2 m) Circular Reservoir

SURFACE
Crushed stone/grass

ROUTE RATING
Route 1 - Easy (inc. Tapping Trail)
Route 2 - Easy adverturous

PROVISION FOR PEOPLE WITH DISABILITIES
Path suitable for wheelchairs, also a 1 km
visually impaired tapping trail around Arley
Reservoir. Toilet facilities

NO DOGS ALLOWED

Worthington Lakes Environmental Education Centre is situated north of Wigan and south of Chorley on the A5016. The Leeds & Liverpool Canal lies to the east and the town of Standish to the west.

The Douglas Valley is a picturesque setting for enjoying the varied trails around the park and the Lakes. The River Douglas, which has its source on Winter Hill, winds its way through the beautiful area of Arley Woods with its coniferous trees and wonderful wild flowers. The river then disappears into a half mile tunnel, which was built in the mid 1800's to change the course of the river, allowing Worthington Lakes to be built. The Douglas River reappears at the southern end of the park ending its journey in the Irish Sea.

The 'Lakes' are made up of three reservoirs, the most northerly one Adlington, has a nature reserve situated at the far end of it, the middle reservoir is Arley with a circular walk that can also be accessed by people with disabilities, including a tapping rail for people who are visually impaired. The most southerly reservoir is Worthington where the Education Centre is situated.

The Douglas Valley and Adlington Park have an amazing and varied amount of wildfowl including the Great Crested Grebe and the Ruddy Duck with its powder blue bill, also the kingfisher with its piping call can be seen near the feeder stream beside Arley reservoir.

Kingfisher and yellow King Cups

Please note that due to Worthington Lakes being a working site providing drinking water no dogs are allowed in the park, except Guide Dogs.

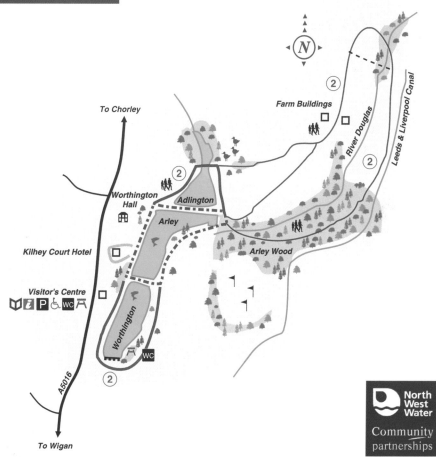

GAMBLESIDE

START & FINISH
Car Park beside the dam of Clowbridge Reservoir

MAP
O/S Outdoor Leisure 21 (South Pennines)

LENGTH (approx)
3 ¼ km (2 m) Circular
Route 2 - 1 km (½m) Linear (continuation of shore path)

SURFACE
Grass/stone

ROUTE RATING
Easy adventurous

PROVISION FOR PEOPLE WITH DISABILITIES
Not suitable for wheelchairs

The Clowbridge reservoir is situated to the east of the A682 Manchester Road between Burnley and Rawtenstall beside the hamlet of Clow Bridge.

The Gambleside Trail is a well defined route clearly waymarked with extensive views across the moorland. Ancient trading routes across these moors were used by packhorse trains which passed through the hamlet of Gambleside regularly, carrying woollen cloth from Rochdale to the Ribble valley

The earliest record of Gambleside goes back to 1242 where it was listed as one of eleven of the vaccaries or cow pastures in Rossendale where 70 to 80 head of cattle would graze. Much lime was carried by pack horse which gives its name to the river in the valley Limey Water. There were many pits in the area as the demand for coal grew to feed the steam powered cotton industry.

Near the ruined site of Gambleside an open air baptistry can be seen which was fed by the stream coming off the moorland.

Site of the former Hamlet of Gambleside with reservoir in the background.

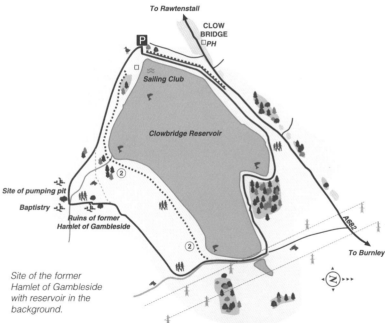

EQUIPMENT NOTE: It is advisable to wear sturdy boots and carry waterproofs.

Waterskiing

Cowm Reservoir is situated to the west of Whitworth and the A671 Rochdale to Bacup road.

The valley's natural fauna and wildlife beside the path around the reservoir makes this route very pleasant and a relaxing one to follow.

Although the valley of Cowm is quite desolate today with few trees or water fowl it was not always been the case. The first homesteads settled in 1566 and by 1851 there was a thriving community.

COWM RESERVOIR

START & FINISH
off Market Street, Whitworth - up Tong Lane to Tong End - Way marked route

MAP
O/S Outdoor Leisure 21 (South Pennines)

LENGTH (approx)
2 km (1 ¼ m) Circular
Route 2 - 5 km (3m) Circular

SURFACE
Gravel /grass

ROUTE RATING
Easy

PROVISION FOR PEOPLE WITH DISABILITIES
Path suitable for wheelchairs also disabled cyclists. Water Ski Centre. Toilet facilities.

With the reservoir being 250 metres above sea level there can be a fair breeze sweeping down the valley, which is one reason why the Whitworth Waterski Association chose the reservoir as a watersport centre for disabled and able-bodied people.

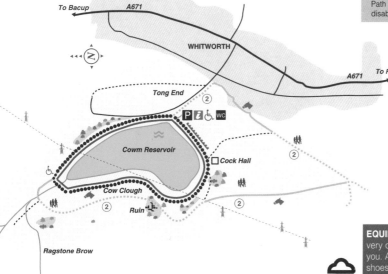

EQUIPMENT NOTE: The mist can roll over the hills very quickly, be sure to have a waterproof jacket with you. As the walk is on one level a pair of comfortable shoes/boots or strong trainers would be adequate.

North West Water
Community partnerships

BLACK MOSS RESERVOIRS

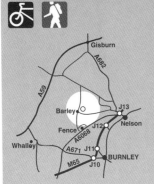

START & FINISH
Car park in Barley

MAP
O/S Outdoor Leisure 41 (Forest of Bowland)

LENGTH (approx)
5 km (3m) Circular
Route 2 - 5 km (3m) Circular

SURFACE
Stoney/grass

ROUTE RATING
Moderate Adverturous

PROVISION FOR PEOPLE WITH DISABILITIES
Not suitable for wheelchairs

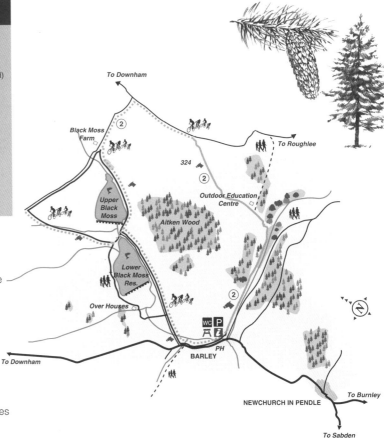

Black Moss Reservoirs are situated to the east of Pendle Hill and Clitheroe and west of Barrowford and the A682. Gisburn is to the north and the village of Newchurch in Pendle is to the south.

The two Black Moss Reservoirs provide drinking water for Nelson. The upper reservoir was completed in 1894, and the lower one in 1903. The majority of the wooded plantations have been planted with different varieties of spruce, sitka and beech trees. Aitken Wood planted in 1935 is the largest woodland around Barley.

The first route around the two reservoirs has a good gravel path around most of the trail with scenic views across the water.

The second route is inclined to be boggy if the weather has been inclement, as it traces footpaths over fields and goes along the bank of the river. A very exciting and enjoyable route.

EQUIPMENT NOTE: The mist can roll over the hills very quickly, be sure to have a waterproof jacket with you. It is advisable to wear sturdy boots.

endle Hill with the Ogden Reservoirs at the foot are situated ast of Clitheroe and the A59, and rest of Barrowford and the A682. he village of Sabden is to the outh and Gisburn in the north.

Barley, in 1324 was known as Barelegh' meaning infertile meadow. he township earned its livelihood in the 18th century from the manufacture of textiles and the use of handlooms in the houses as a source of extra income.

The route around Upper and Lower Ogden Reservoirs, which supply drinking water for the Nelson area, is a very pleasant one with the long "hump back" of Pendle Hill on one side and Ogden Brook and the woodlands on the other. The second route goes up Ogden Clough to the 'Big End' of Pendle and returns down Boar Clough.

This is an exciting circular walk on Pendle Hill - which at its highest point is 1830 ft (563 mtrs), the views are magnificent in every direction.

OGDEN RESERVOIRS & PENDLE HILL

START & FINISH
Car park in Barley

MAP
O/S Outdoor Leisure 41 (Forest of Bowland)

LENGTH (approx)
Route 1 - Ogden Res. 5 km (3 m)
Route 2 - Pendle Hill 11 km (7 m)
Both routes - Circular

SURFACE
Stoney/moorland grass

ROUTE RATING
Route 1 - Moderate
Route 2 - Hard Adventurous

PROVISION FOR PEOPLE WITH DISABILITIES
Not suitable for wheelchairs

EQUIPMENT NOTE: The mist can roll over the hills very quickly, it is advisable to carry waterproofs and wear sturdy boots.

North West Water

Community partnerships

JUMBLES

START & FINISH
Car Park at Waterfold, Jumbles Reservoir.

MAP
O/S Explorer No. 19 (West Pennine Moor)

LENGTH (approx)
4 ½ km (2 ¾ m)
Route 2 - 5 ½ km (3 ⅓ m) Circular

SURFACE
Gravel/grass

ROUTE RATING
Moderate

PROVISION FOR PEOPLE WITH DISABILITIES
Path suitable for wheelchairs. Toilet facilities

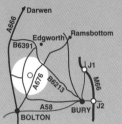

Jumbles Reservoir is situated north of Bolton and west of Ramsbottom and Bury. The A676 is to the east of the reservoir.

The trail goes around the reservoir, which lies over 130 metres above sea level. Jumbles Reservoir was opened in 1971 and displays a magnificent vast grassed embankment which holds back the waters. It is the most southerly and newest of the three reservoirs in Bradshaw Valley.

There is a wealth of wild vegetation along the banks of the reservoir including wild orchids. The wooded areas include silver birch and oak trees. The water from the reservoir is slowed down by large stone blocks in the water channel where you may be rewarded by seeing a grey wagtail, dipper or even a kingfisher.

EQUIPMENT NOTE: It is advisable to wear sturdy boots and take a waterproof jacket.

TURTON BOTTOMS

Turton Tower

To Holco & Bur

Torra Barn

Quarries (dis.)

Sailing Club

Jumbles Res.

Hide

WC

Last Drop Village

BROMLEY CROSS

A676

N

To Bolton

Worsthorne Moor is situated east of Burnley and the villages of Worsthorne and Hurstwood. The reservoirs of Hurstwood and Cant Clough are on the Moor, north of the road known as 'The Long Causeway' between Burnley and Hebden Bridge.

The route around Hurstwood Reservoir, which was built in 1925, has panoramic views of the open moorland and contrasts with the softer beauty of the trail along Rock Water, before continuing the walk up to the dam on Cant Clough Reservoir (built in 1876).

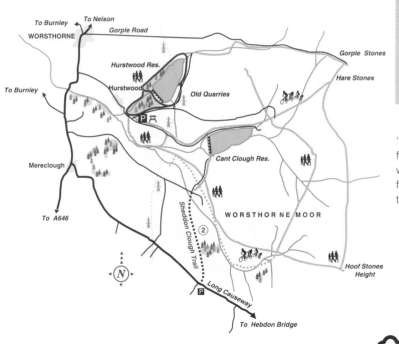

The second trail is the 'Shedden Clough Trail' famous for being a packhorse route, where mules would carry lime from the opencast mining twenty miles away to the Burnley area for using as a fertiliser and making mortar for building. The ground is very uneven due to the worn stone of the trail.

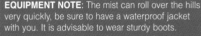

EQUIPMENT NOTE: The mist can roll over the hills very quickly, be sure to have a waterproof jacket with you. It is advisable to wear sturdy boots.

North West Water
Community partnerships

ANGLEZARKE

START & FINISH
Car Park beside Anglezarke Reservoir

MAP
O/S Explorer 19 (West Pennine Moor)

LENGTH (approx)
Woodland Trail - 3 km (2 m) Circular

SURFACE
Gravel

ROUTE RATING
Moderate

PROVISION FOR PEOPLE WITH DISABILITIES
Path suitable for accompanied wheelchairs

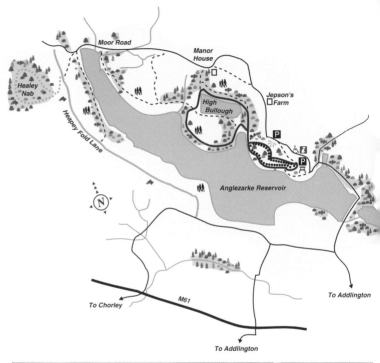

Anglezarke and High Bullough Reservoirs are situated north of Lever Park and Rivington. To the east is Anglezarke Moor to the west is the M61 and the town of Chorley.

The Woodland Trail passes through woodland areas as well as following a section of the path beside the two reservoirs. Most of the beech and oak trees are over a 100 years-old.

Anglezarke Reservoir was built in 1857 as part of a chain of reservoirs in the Rivington area. It is one of the largest reservoirs in Lancashire, whereas High Bullough Reservoir is one of the smallest. Both reservoirs are important feeding grounds for large flocks of wildfowl.

Lower Rivington Reservoir

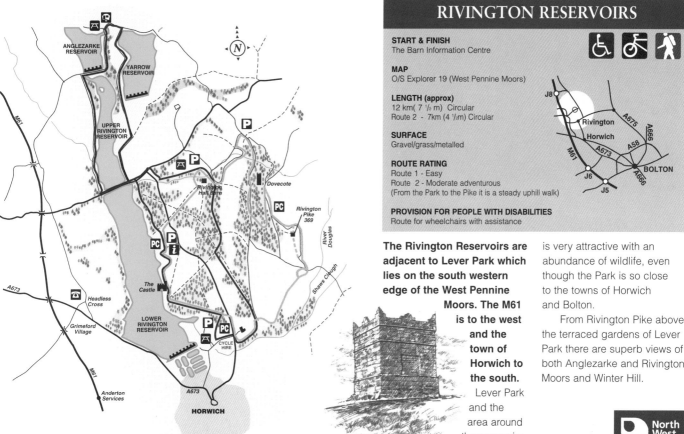

RIVINGTON RESERVOIRS

START & FINISH
The Barn Information Centre

MAP
O/S Explorer 19 (West Pennine Moors)

LENGTH (approx)
12 km(7 ½ m) Circular
Route 2 - 7km (4 ½m) Circular

SURFACE
Gravel/grass/metalled

ROUTE RATING
Route 1 - Easy
Route 2 - Moderate adventurous
(From the Park to the Pike it is a steady uphill walk)

PROVISION FOR PEOPLE WITH DISABILITIES
Route for wheelchairs with assistance

The Rivington Reservoirs are adjacent to Lever Park which lies on the south western edge of the West Pennine Moors. The M61 is to the west and the town of Horwich to the south. Lever Park and the area around the reservoirs is very attractive with an abundance of wildlife, even though the Park is so close to the towns of Horwich and Bolton.

From Rivington Pike above the terraced gardens of Lever Park there are superb views of both Anglezarke and Rivington Moors and Winter Hill.

Rivington Pike

North West Water
Community partnerships

LUNE RIVERSIDE PARK

START & FINISH
Caton Green or Crook O'Lune car parks

MAP
O/S Landra)nger 97
(Kendal and Morecambe)

SURFACE
Gravel/grass/metalled

ROUTE RATING
Easy

PROVISION FOR PEOPLE WITH DISABILITIES
Disabled gates and wheelchair route.

Lune Riverside Park is situated between Lancaster and Bull Beck on the banks of the River Lune, east of the M6.

The Lancaster to Bull Beck leisure and cycle trail, the route of the old Lancaster-Wennington railway line, runs parallel to the Riverside Park and the River Lune.

The Riverside Park on the Crook O'Lune is an area of woodland and meadow of great beauty. One path takes you down to the water's edge where you can watch, amongst other wildfowl the unusual sight of coastal birds such as Oystercatchers and Ringed Plover, which don't normally venture this far inland.

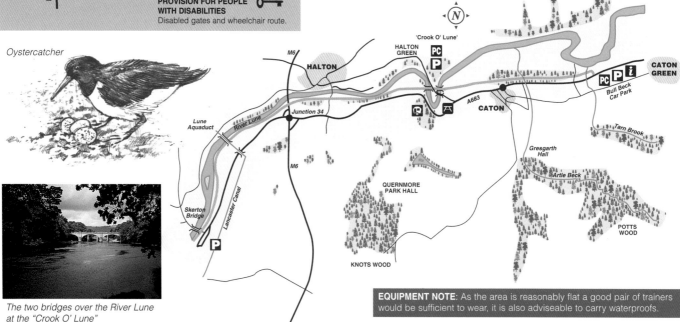

Oystercatcher

The two bridges over the River Lune at the "Crook O' Lune"

EQUIPMENT NOTE: As the area is reasonably flat a good pair of trainers would be sufficient to wear, it is also adviseable to carry waterproofs.

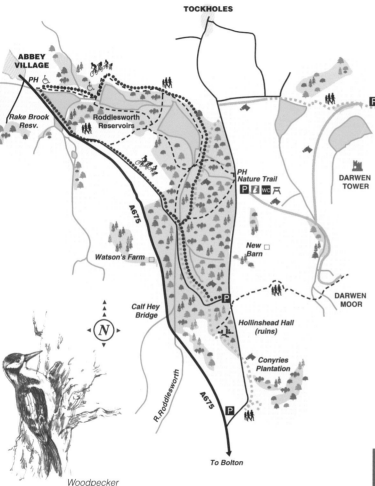

TOCKHOLES

ABBEY VILLAGE

PH

Rake Brook Resv.

Roddlesworth Reservoirs

A675

PH
Nature Trail
P i WC

DARWEN TOWER

New Barn

Watson's Farm

A675

Calf Hey Bridge

DARWEN MOOR

Hollinshead Hall (ruins)

R.Roddlesworth

Conyries Plantation

A675

P

To Bolton

N

Woodpecker

TOCKHOLES AND DARWEN

START & FINISH
Car park at Roddlesworth Information Centre

MAP
O/S Explorer 19 (West Pennine Moors)

LENGTH (approx)
Various routes of differing lengths

SURFACE
Woodland/grass/gravel

ROUTE RATING
Moderate

PROVISION FOR PEOPLE WITH DISABILITIES
Path suitable for wheelchairs. Toilet facilities

BLACKBURN

A674

M65   J3

A674   Darwen

J8   A674   Withnell   A666

M61   A675   Tockholes

Roddlesworth Reservoirs lie within the Tockholes Plantations, to the south is Brown Hill and Withnell Moor, to the east is the town of Darwen and the M65 to the north. The A675 runs down the western edge of the trails area.

There is a network of trails within the Tockholes area around the reservoirs and in the wooded plantations. The area within the woodland can be fairly hilly. The trees were planted originally to help stabilise the soil and stop erosion caused by the river running too quickly down the valley. This woodland area has produced a wonderful breeding ground for wild birds and animals. Woodpeckers can frequently be heard tapping on the trees looking for insects.

EQUIPMENT NOTE: It is recommended to take waterproofs with you, also wear a pair of sturdy shoes or boots.

North West Water
Community partnerships

TURTON, ENTWISTLE & WAYOH RES.

START & FINISH
Entwistle Car park for both reservoir routes

MAP
O/S Explorer 19 (West Pennine Moors)

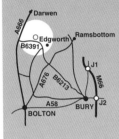

LENGTH (approx)
Turton Res. 4 km (2 ½m)
Route 2 - Wayoh Res. 5 km (3 m)

SURFACE
Gravel/grass

ROUTE RATING
Easy

PROVISION FOR PEOPLE WITH DISABILITIES
Path suitable for wheelchairs around Turton &
Entwistle Reservoir.
South side - Easy
North side - Easy adventurous

These two reservoirs are situated north of Bolton, and east of the A666. To the west is Holcombe Moor and Jumbles Reservoir is to the south.

Construction of Entwistle reservoir began in 1831, where the waters assisted in the cleaning and bleaching of wool and cotton in the local mills. Together with Wayoh, the two reservoirs make up around 50% of Bolton's drinking water.

With a combination of tall fir trees, moorland and long stretches of water, Entwistle reservoir has a wild beauty. The northerly section of Wayoh is a nature reserve, where there is a variety of wildfowl.

There is very little wildlife around Entwistle due mainly to the tall coniferous trees leaving the ground cover very dark. Nevertheless violets and marsh marigolds are widespread in spring. Fairy

Battery to the north end of Turton & Entwistle Reservoir is the name given to an outcrop of rock, very popular with rock climbers. During the 17th century the 'Battery' known locally as 'Pulpit Rock' was used as a secret meeting place for non-conformist worshippers as they were forbidden by law to worship and had to seek out secret locations.

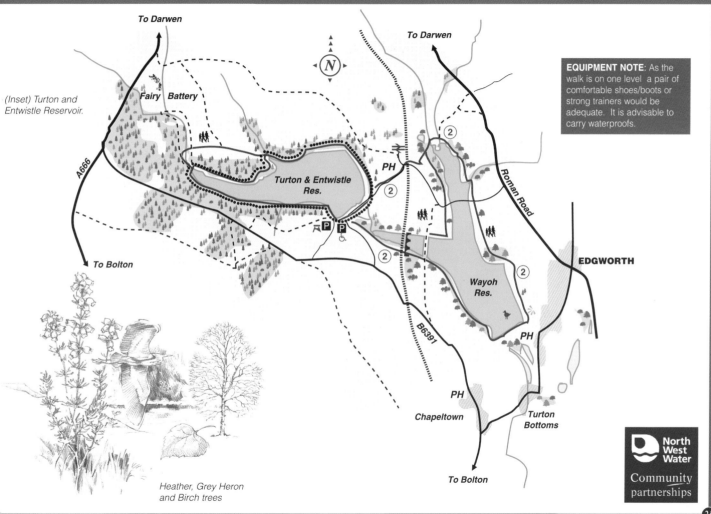

To Darwen

To Darwen

(Inset) Turton and Entwistle Reservoir.

Fairy Battery

A666

To Bolton

Turton & Entwistle Res.

EQUIPMENT NOTE: As the walk is on one level a pair of comfortable shoes/boots or strong trainers would be adequate. It is advisable to carry waterproofs.

Roman Road

PH

EDGWORTH

Wayoh Res.

B6391

PH

Chapeltown

PH

Turton Bottoms

To Bolton

Heather, Grey Heron and Birch trees

North West Water

Community partnerships

25

CALF HEY RESERVOIR
Haslingden Grane

PROVISION FOR PEOPLE WITH DISABILITIES
Suitable path with accompaniment. ('RADAR' Key required) Toilet facilities at Clough Head Car Park (Grane Road B6232).

START & FINISH
Calf Hey Car Park

MAP
O/S Explorer 19 (West Pennine Moor)

LENGTH (approx)
2 km (1 1/4 m) Circular (Calf Hey Trail)
Route 2 - 4 km (2 1/2m) Circular (Whisky Trail)

SURFACE
Calf Hey Trail - crushed stone
Other routes - grass/stone

ROUTE RATING
Calf Hey Trail - Easy adventurous
Other routes - Moderate adventurous

Calf Hey is situated west of Rawtenstall and the A56, with Musbury Heights to the south and Haslingden Moor and the B6232 to Blackburn to the north.

Calf Hey is one of three reservoirs in the Haslingden Grane Valley. Construction was completed in 1859 to supply drinking water to Bury and Radcliffe.

The first route is around Calf Hey Reservoir which has a metalled and gravel path and is easy to walk for people with disabilities. On route you will pass through the ruins of Hartley House and cottages. In the 1800's there was a thriving handloom cottage industry on this site until the invention of steam powered looms made hand weaving uneconomical. At the ruins of Lower Ormerods, you can see part of the staircase, wall cupboards and also the loomshop attached at the rear. The car park stands on the site of Chapel Row which was once part of Grane village. At the end of the car park there is a small graveyard. Grane methodist chapel, built in 1815, stood in this area.

Before the construction of Ogden Reservoir in 1912 and the flooding of the area, the church of St. Stephens was demolished and rebuilt further down the valley.

The second route takes in the ruins of three farmsteads, where for many years the occupants earned their living by producing illigally distilled whisky. 'The Whisky Spinners' as they were known, carried on their trade for about 150 years making whisky in secret chambers and passages hidden in the buildings. This walk can be particularly boggy after a spell of wet weather, but the views down the valley more than compensate for muddy ankles.

Calf Hey Reservoir with Haslingden Moor on the sky line.

EQUIPMENT NOTE: The mist can roll over the hills very quickly, be sure to have a waterproof jacket with you. A pair of comfortable shoes/boots for the higher level paths.

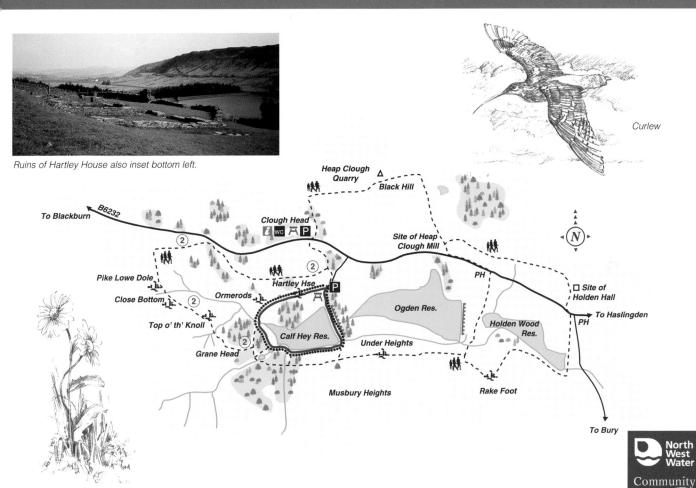

Ruins of Hartley House also inset bottom left.

Curlew

Heap Clough Quarry

Black Hill

To Blackburn

B6232

2

Clough Head

i WC P

Site of Heap Clough Mill

2

Pike Lowe Dole

Hartley Hse

PH

Close Bottom

2

Ormerods

P

Site of Holden Hall

To Haslingden

Top o' th' Knoll

Ogden Res.

Holden Wood Res.

PH

2

Grane Head

Calf Hey Res.

Under Heights

Musbury Heights

Rake Foot

To Bury

One Eyed Daisies

N

North West Water

Community partnerships

27

WALVERDEN

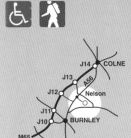

START
Route 1 & Route 2 - Car park (top of Brunswick Street, Nelson)

FINISH
Route 1 Circular path around Walverden Res.
Route 2 Lower Coldwell Reservoir

MAP
O/S Outdoor Leisure 21 (South Pennines)

LENGTH (approx)
2 km (1 ¼m) Circular
Route 2 - 7 km (4 ½ m) Linear

ROUTE RATING
Route 1 - Easy, but inclined to be muddy
Route 2 - Easy adventurous

SURFACE
Route 1 - Gravel
Route 2 - Gravel/grass/stoney

PROVISION FOR PEOPLE WITH DISABILITIES
Route 1 - suitable for wheelchairs only in the dry season - path too muddy otherwise.

Walverden Reservoir is situated east of Brierfield and south of Nelson. The reservoir is well worth finding. Directions from the Arndale Centre in Nelson - turn on to Netherfield Road and up Brunswick Street through an industrial area and down a track to the Car Park at the base of the reservoir dam.

An exceptional find, a little gem of wildlife conservation , quite a surprise - having come through a very built up industrial area to get to the reservoir.

The wildfowl on the reservoir is extensive for such a small area of water. There is also a hide so that the wildfowl can be watched or photographed. Geese both white and Canadian, Mallards and Crested Grebe can often be seen. Coarse fishing with very good facilities for anglers - permits can be obtained from the Bailiff at the reservoir.

The second route to Lower Coldwell reservoir is a longer trail over the hill from Lower Fenny Moor Foot and through Catlow Bottoms. Should you feel very energetic follow the Bronte Way to Wycoller!

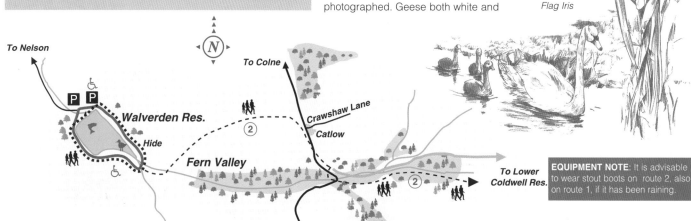

Swans and Flag Iris

EQUIPMENT NOTE: It is advisable to wear stout boots on route 2, also on route 1, if it has been raining.

North West Water

Community partnerships

MACCLESFIELD FOREST

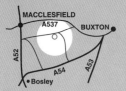

START & FINISH
Car Park opposite Trentabank Reservoir
Waymarked with 'Yellow Arrows'

MAP
O/S Outdoor Leisure 21 (South Pennines)

LENGTH (approx)
(1) 1 km (½ m)   Linear (for wheelchairs)
(2) 5 km (3 m)   Circular) Forest
(3) 9 km (5 ½ m) Circular) waymarked routes

**PROVISION FOR PEOPLE
WITH DISABILITIES**
A short wheelchair trail beside
Trentabank Reservoir. Toilet facilities.

SURFACE
Woodland/grass/tarmac

ROUTE RATING
(1) Easy   (2) Moderate   (3) Hard

Macclesfield Forest is situated east of Macclesfield and west of the Goyt Valley. The A537 is to the north and the A54 to the south.

The forest is a working area and as the timber is felled and replanted, the woodland scenery is always in a state of change. Therefore the paths may be closed temporarily, so please follow the forestry waymarked trail numbers at all times.

There are four reservoirs in the vicinity. The Ridgegate and Trentabank reservoirs within the forest provide the Macclesfield area with drinking water.

The present Macclesfield Forest Chapel dates from 1834 when it replaced an earlier chapel dating back to 1673. The dates recording these events are over the doorway. The chapel is built in pink sandstone which had been quarried at Tegg's Nose.

Although the forest has a herd of red deer they are very shy creatures. The holes made by badgers as they forage for insects near fallen logs can be seen. The woodland is renowned for its numerous variety of mosses and fungi including stinkhorns, honey fungus and fly agaric.

The reservoirs are the home for many species of wildfowl. In different seasons there would be tufted duck, and great crested grebe among many others. The larch trees on the shore of Trentabank reservoir are home to the largest heronry in the Peak District.

Woodland glade

EQUIPMENT NOTE: A stout pair of shoes or boots are essential for walks 2 & 3.

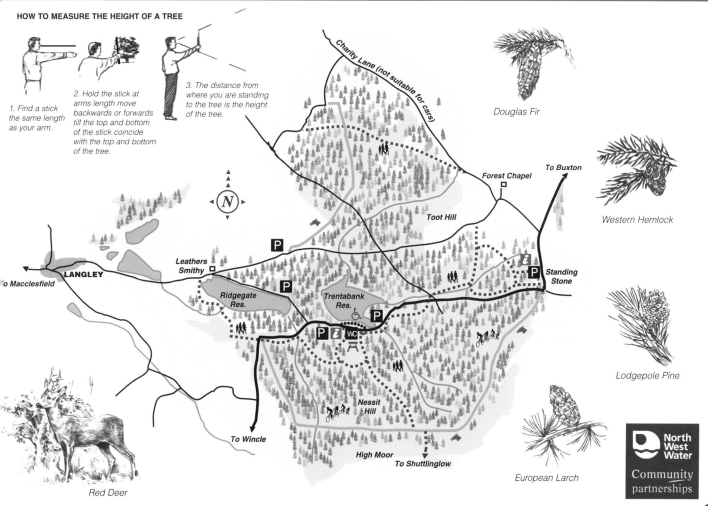

HOW TO MEASURE THE HEIGHT OF A TREE

1. Find a stick the same length as your arm.

2. Hold the stick at arms length move backwards or forwards till the top and bottom of the stick coincide with the top and bottom of the tree.

3. The distance from where you are standing to the tree is the height of the tree.

Charity Lane (not suitable for cars)

Douglas Fir

Western Hemlock

Forest Chapel

To Buxton

Toot Hill

N

Leathers Smithy

Standing Stone

Ridgegate Res.

Trentabank Res.

WC

Lodgepole Pine

To Macclesfield

LANGLEY

Nessit Hill

To Wincle

High Moor

To Shuttlinglow

European Larch

Red Deer

North West Water

Community partnerships

31

DOVE STONE

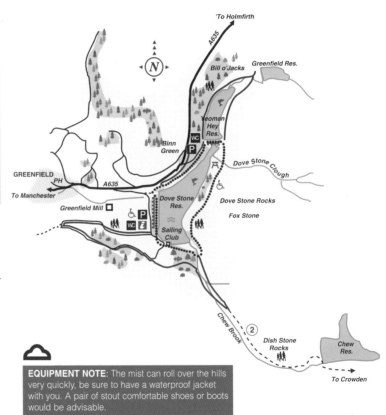

START & FINISH
Car Park near the dam on Yeoman
Hey Reservoir

MAP
O/S Outdoor Leisure 1
(The Peak District, Dark Peak)

LENGTH (APPROX)
4 km (2 1/2m) Circular
(Dove Stone Reservoir - wheelchair route)
Route 2 - 3 km (2m) Linear (Chew Reservoir)

SURFACE
Stone/grass

ROUTE RATING
Easy to hard (depending on route taken)

PROVISION FOR PEOPLE WITH DISABILITIES
An anti-clockwise path around Dove Stone
Reservoir for accompanied wheelchairs.
Toilet facilities.

Dove Stone is situated in the Peak District National Park, east of Oldham and Ashton-under-Lyne on Saddleworth Moor. To the north is Diggle and Upper Mill, and the A635 runs to the west of the reservoirs.

In Dove Stone valley there are four reservoirs. Yeoman Hey is the oldest reservoir, constructed in 1880. All the reservoirs supply water to the outskirts of Manchester. Chew, the most southerly, was at its time of construction in 1914, the highest reservoir in the British Isles - 1600ft above sea level. A tramway was constructed to transport material to the site and it is this tramway that route two follows from Dove Stone. Some of the tramway bed is still visible.

Dove Stone valley is surrounded by bleak moorland and high outcrops of rock giving a magnificent panoramic view of the southern Pennines.

Most of the older woodland is a variety of spruce and pine, but more recently several broad leaf species have been included in the plantations to help provide a habitat for a larger range of wildlife.

EQUIPMENT NOTE: The mist can roll over the hills very quickly, be sure to have a waterproof jacket with you. A pair of stout comfortable shoes or boots would be advisable.

Watergrove Reservoir is situated north of Wardle and the A58 Halifax Road and south of Bacup. Rochdale is to the west and Littleborough to the east.

Watergrove Reservoir was built in the 1930's. Rochdale Corporation chose Watergrove as a suitable site to build a large reservoir, due mainly to a prolonged drought. The ruins of the old village of Watergrove lie under the large expanse of water, and above the reservoir dotted around the landscape there are several ruins originally belonging to the submerged village.

Set into the reservoir wall 100 mtrs from the car park, there are a number of datestones, drinking troughs and window mullions rescued from the old Watergrove Village.

WATERGROVE TRAILS

START & FINISH
Car Park under the dam on Ramsden Road, Wardle

MAP
O/S Outdoor Leisure 21 (South Pennines)

LENGTH (approx)
Watergrove Trail 3 km (2 m)
Route 2 - Hades Trail 6½ km (4 m)

SURFACE
Both routes grass/stoney can be very boggy

ROUTE RATING
Watergrove - Moderate
Hades - Hard

PROVISION FOR PEOPLE WITH DISABILITIES
Not suitable for wheelchairs

The first route 'The Watergrove Trail around the reservoir is mostly of good surface although it can be boggy in places as it follows the perimeter of the reservoir and goes past the sailing club.

The second route 'Hades Trail', going up to the ruins of Higher Slack Brook Farm, can be very boggy particularly in the walled sunken lanes around the reservoir.

The Long Causeway, an old packhorse route to Ramsden branches off at the northerly point of this route.

North West Water
Community partnerships

To Whitworth

Brown Wardle

Middle Hill

High Wardle

Roads Farm

Hades

To Rochdale

N

Watergrove Res.

Sailboard Club
WC

Higher Slack Brook Farm

Little Town

PH
PH

WARDLE

Crook Farm

To Todmorden

Hospital

A58

Dobbin Hill

To Shaw

To Littleborough

EQUIPMENT NOTE: The mist can roll over the hills very quickly, be sure to have a waterproof jacket with you. Due to the many streams, it is recommended that you wear sturdy boots for both routes.

BACUP   A681

Whitworth
A671
Wardle
ROCHDALE   Littleborough
B6225
A58   A664
A627(M)   M62

GOYT VALLEY

START & FINISH
Car Park at The Street - north western end of Errwood Reservoir. Car Park at Goyts Lane (2) for wheelchair route

MAP
O/S Outdoor Leisure 24
(The Peak District, White Peak)

LENGTH (approx)
Various routes of differing lengths

SURFACE
Stone/grass/metalled

ROUTE RATING
Moderate adventurous

PROVISION FOR PEOPLE WITH DISABILITIES
(1) Along the western bank of Errwood Reservoir.
The metalled road to Derbyshire Bridge
(see notice boards for times of road closure)
(2) Goyts Lane - along the route of the former
Cromford and High Peak Railway - very peaceful.

Route for wheelchairs - ONE WAY road denoted by GREEN DOTS The Goyt Valley is situated within the Peak District National Park east of the A5004 Whaley Bridge to Buxton road. To the south lies Goyt's Moss and to the north the village of Fernilee. The western side of the valley is flanked by Shining Tor (1833') and Cats Tor (1703')

The Goyt was once the separation between the Royle Forest of the Peak to the east and Macclesfield Forest to the west, where following the Norman Conquest, extensive strips of countryside were reserved for hunting game

From the Errwood Reservoir dam the view of the valley, in either direction, with its two reservoirs is magnificent.

In 1830, the Cromford and High Peak Railway was built to link the Peak Forest Canal with the Cromford Canal and the road up Bunsal Incline follows the former track which disappears into a tunnel in the direction of Buxton. The small reservoirs near the road were built to provide water to assist the steam engines to climb this steep ascent.

The gritstone quarry of Goyts Clough was, in the 17th century, the birth place of Pickford's removal company and Errwood Hall which is now a ruin, was built by the Grimshawe family in 1830 with impressive grounds of exceptional beauty planted with rhododendron, azalea bushes and dense pinewoods.

Jenkin Chapel

Forest glade

Fernilee reservoir looking north

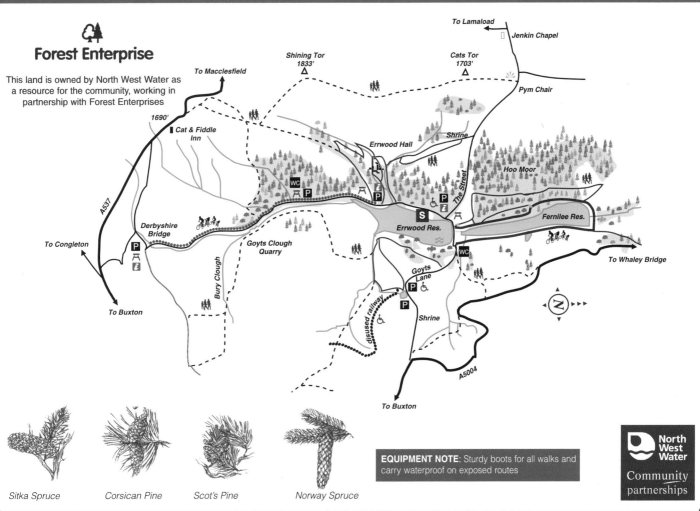

Forest Enterprise

This land is owned by North West Water as a resource for the community, working in partnership with Forest Enterprises

To Lamaload

Jenkin Chapel

To Macclesfield

Shining Tor 1833'

Cats Tor 1703'

Pym Chair

1690'

Cat & Fiddle Inn

Errwood Hall

Shrine

Hoo Moor

A537

Derbyshire Bridge

Goyts Clough Quarry

Bury Clough

WC

Errwood Res.

The Street

Ferniley Res.

To Congleton

To Buxton

disused railway

Goyts Lane

WC

Shrine

To Whaley Bridge

N

To Buxton

A5004

Sitka Spruce

Corsican Pine

Scot's Pine

Norway Spruce

EQUIPMENT NOTE: Sturdy boots for all walks and carry waterproof on exposed routes

North West Water

Community partnerships

PIETHORNE VALLEY

START & FINISH
Car Park at Spring Mill near Ogden Reservoir

MAP
O/S Outdoor Leisure 21 (South Pennines)

LENGTH (approx)
Route 1 - 2 ½ km (1 ½ m)
Route 2 - 4 ½ km (2 ¾ m)
Route 3 - 5 ½ km (3 ½ m)
All routes circular

SURFACE
Stoney/grass/metalled

ROUTE RATING
(1) Easy   (2) Moderate   (3) Hard

PROVISION FOR PEOPLE WITH DISABILITIES
A route along Waterworks Road is suitable for wheelchairs.   Toilet facilities. Car Parking beside Piethorne and Ogden Reservoirs.

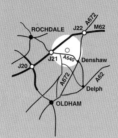

Piethorne Valley is situated on the A640 between Newhey and Denshaw. Rochdale and the M62 are to the north, Oldham is to the south.

The first route around Ogden, the most southerly reservoir in the valley, is an easy stroll round the expanse of water and past the ruin of Rag Hole Farm. Ogden reservoir was commissioned in 1878 to collect water from Wickenhall Brook to provide drinking water for Oldham. Rag Hole Farm in the 1850's was a thriving farmstead probably growing rye and barley.

The second trail goes round both Kitciffe and Piethorne Reservoirs and by-passes the Bluebell Wood Nature Reserve where beech, rowan and sycamore trees have been planted, providing valuable habitat for wild animals sheltering off the high moor.

The third route is the most southerly, keeping on the road past all three reservoirs, the route commences opposite the dam on Hanging Lees Reservoir. This walk takes you past Rooden reservoir, one of the deepest reservoirs at 79ft. Both the villages of Lower and Upper Ogden contain houses built from local gritstone dating back to 1710. On the high moor above Ogden Edge there are many different breeds of sheep, all very hardy to cope with the climate changes on the Pennines.

Ogden Reservoir

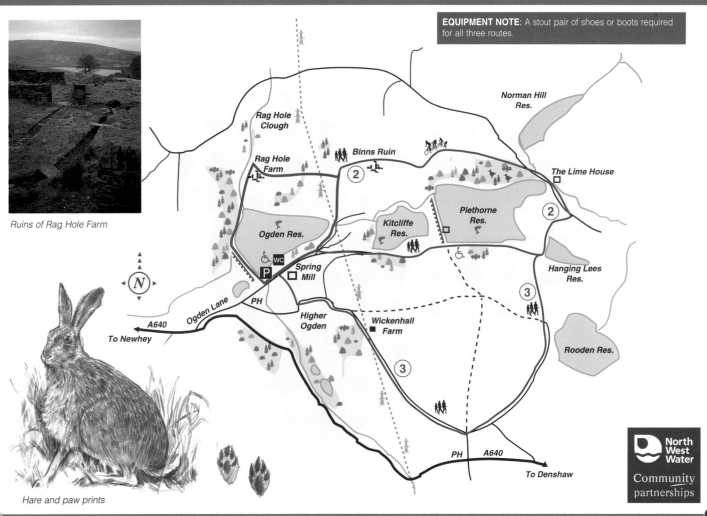

EQUIPMENT NOTE: A stout pair of shoes or boots required for all three routes.

Ruins of Rag Hole Farm

Rag Hole Clough

Binns Ruin

Rag Hole Farm

Norman Hill Res.

The Lime House

②

Piethorne Res.

Kitcliffe Res.

Ogden Res.

Hanging Lees Res.

③

WC

P

Spring Mill

Higher Ogden

Wickenhall Farm

Rooden Res.

③

Ogden Lane

PH

A640

To Newhey

PH   A640

To Denshaw

N

Hare and paw prints

North West Water

Community partnerships

37

THE LONGDENDALE TRAIL
Upper Longdendale Valley

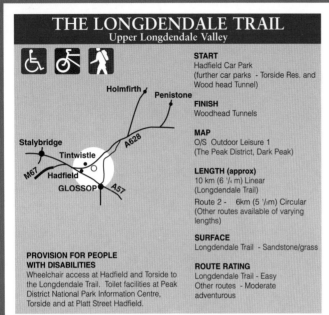

START
Hadfield Car Park
(further car parks - Torside Res. and Wood head Tunnel)

FINISH
Woodhead Tunnels

MAP
O/S Outdoor Leisure 1
(The Peak District, Dark Peak)

LENGTH (approx)
10 km (6 $\frac{1}{4}$ m) Linear
(Longdendale Trail)

Route 2 -   6km (5 $\frac{1}{2}$m) Circular
(Other routes available of varying lengths)

SURFACE
Longdendale Trail - Sandstone/grass

ROUTE RATING
Longdendale Trail - Easy
Other routes - Moderate adventurous

PROVISION FOR PEOPLE WITH DISABILITIES
Wheelchair access at Hadfield and Torside to the Longdendale Trail. Toilet facilities at Peak District National Park Information Centre, Torside and at Platt Street Hadfield.

The Longdendale Trail is situated in the Upper Longdendale Valley, within The Peak District National Park. South of the A628 and north of the town of Glossop.
The Longdendale Trail takes you along part of the route of the old Great Central Manchester Sheffield Railway.

It is a very picturesque valley with its five reservoirs surrounded by high moorland. The reservoirs were completed in 1877 and were the largest artificial expanse of water in the world at that time.

The first route is along the 'Longdendale Trail', a leisure route for horse riders, on their own path, cyclists, walkers and, with assistance, wheelchair users. This trail is part of the Sustrans 'Trans Pennine Trail' which will eventually go from Liverpool to Hull.

The second route is a circular route commencing from Crowden. From the car park, use the Pennine Way path to start this route, then up over Rakes Moss to Chew Reservoir, and returning via Tintwistle Knarr Quarry and Lad's Leap. This route is quite spectacular with its panoramic view of Bleaklow and Longdendale Valley below.

Wildlife in the area includes foxes and hares up on the moors, woodpeckers and flycatchers in the woodland and Canadian Geese and swans on the reservoirs.

European Larch, squirrel and foxgloves

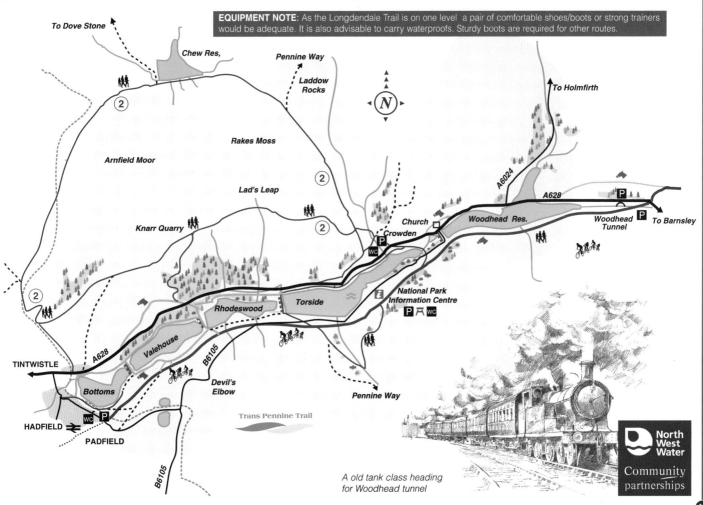

To Dove Stone

Chew Res,

Pennine Way

Laddow Rocks

N

Rakes Moss

Arnfield Moor

To Holmfirth

Lad's Leap

A6024

A628

Woodhead Res,

Knarr Quarry

Church

Crowden

WC

Woodhead Tunnel

To Barnsley

Torside

National Park Information Centre

Rhodeswood

Valehouse

A628

B6105

Bottoms

Devil's Elbow

Pennine Way

TINTWISTLE

HADFIELD

PADFIELD

WC P

Trans Pennine Trail

B6105

A old tank class heading for Woodhead tunnel

North West Water

Community partnerships

LAMALOAD

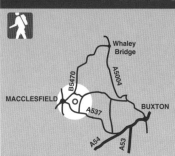

START & FINISH
Lamaload Car Park

MAP
O/S Outdoor Leisure 24
(The Peak District, White Peak)

LENGTH (approx)
1 ½ km (2m) Circular

SURFACE
Stone/grass/metalled

ROUTE RATING
Easy adventurous

**PROVISION FOR PEOPLE
WITH DISABILITIES**
Not suitable for wheelchairs.

NOTE
The Toilets are only open in the summer months.

Lamaload Reservoir is situated north of the A54 Buxton to Macclesfield road within The Peak District National Park. To the east is the Goyt Valley with Macclesfield to the west.

The reservoir at Lamaload was completed in 1964 and supplies drinking water for Macclesfield.

The reservoir is approximately 1000ft (308m) above sea level. The landscape around Lamaload is moorland with a few plantations of larch and pine. The broad leaved woodlands surrounding these plantations provide a habitat for a variety of wildlife.

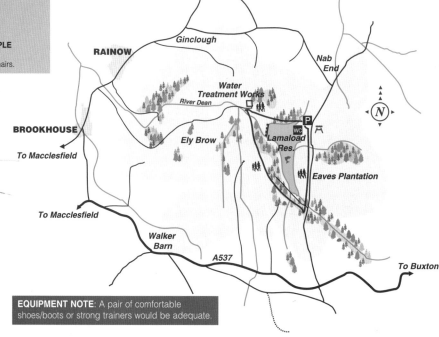

Gorse and Grouse

EQUIPMENT NOTE: A pair of comfortable shoes/boots or strong trainers would be adequate.

Swallow's Wood Trail is situated within a Nature Reserve north west of Arnfield Reservoir. West of this trail is Upper Longdendale Valley and to the south is Hollingworth and the A57. There is approximately a ¹/₂ mile walk to the start at Meadowbank Farm.

This trail has many changes of face and character depending on which season the woodland and hill moorland is visited.

The area around the trail was once part of the Hollingworth Hall Estate. The wildlife in the woodland is in abundance and in the summer months many beautiful butterflies can be seen enjoying the meadow buttercups.

Swallow's Wood Trail and the surrounding nature reserve was once the site of the former Hollingworth and Waste Lodge Reservoirs, Built in 1855 the reservoirs were demolished in 1987 leaving the small lake you see today.

To Stalybridge

Site of Hollingworth Hall

Hall Farm

To Manchester

Swallow's Wood

HOLLINGWORTH

Meadowbank Farm

Tameside Trail

Lower Bank

Quarry

Tameside Trail

Middle Bank

Devil's Bridge

Ogden Brook

N

A628

Arnfield Res.

Crossgate Lane

TINTWISTLE

To Sheffield

STRINESDALE

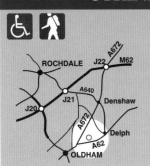

START & FINISH
Car Park at Strinesdale

MAP
O/S Landranger 109 (Manchester)

LENGTH (approx)
Various paths of differing lengths

SURFACE
Gravel/grass/metalled

ROUTE RATING
Easy to Moderate

**PROVISION FOR PEOPLE
WITH DISABILITIES**
Wheelchair route

Strinesdale is situated on the A62 between Oldham and Delph. Rochdale is to the north and Oldham to the south.

Strinesdale is an area of water and woodland covering approximately 40 acres. In 1991, the reservoirs were drained and replaced by two smaller lakes with the old reservoirs being planted with trees and grassland. The original reservoirs were built in 1828 and the date stone can be seen at Upper Strinesdale.

Strinesdale got its name from the Old English 'strine' meaning boundary, as the old Lancashire/Yorkshire boundary ran through the middle of the site.

Herons and kestrels can be seen on the lakeside and as the woodland develops it will provide shelter for animals and birds and many varieties of wild flowers.

EQUIPMENT NOTE: It is recommended that you carry waterproofs and wear either sturdy shoes or boots.

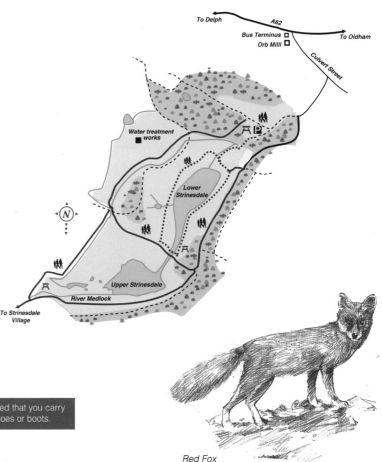

Red Fox

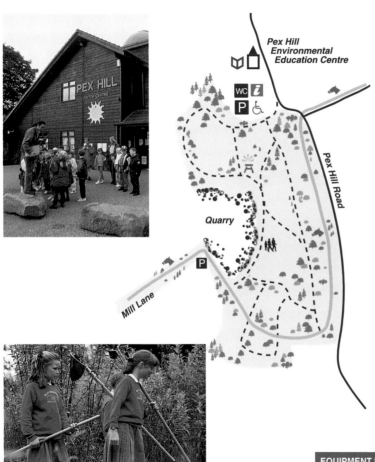

PEX HILL COUNTRY PARK

START & FINISH
Pex Hill Environmental Educational
Centre Car Park

MAP
O/S Landranger 108 (Liverpool)

LENGTH (approx)
Varying lengths according to which path
chosen

SURFACE
Gravel/sandstone

ROUTE RATING
Easy

PROVISION FOR PEOPLE WITH DISABILITIES
Paths suitable for wheelchairs. Toilet facilities.

Pex Hill has situated south of St. Helens and the M62, west of A557, and north of Widnes and the A5080.

Pex Hill has an Environmental Education Centre. It is a 14 acre site on the top of a sandstone hill. The quarry, now disused, provided stone between 1868 and 1876 for building two covered reservoirs, which today provide water for Widnes. It also has an Observatory which is run by the Liverpool Astronomical Society.

The views are tremendous from the picnic area. Cheshire can be seen from across the River Mersey and in the distance Wales and the Clwyd hills.

The Country Park is a haven for wildlife. Walking through the colourful gorse and broom on the moorland and hearing the variety of birds in the oak woodland makes this a delightful route.

North West Water
Community partnerships

EQUIPMENT NOTE: Trainers and sturdy shoes are adequate and it is advisable to take waterproof clothing.

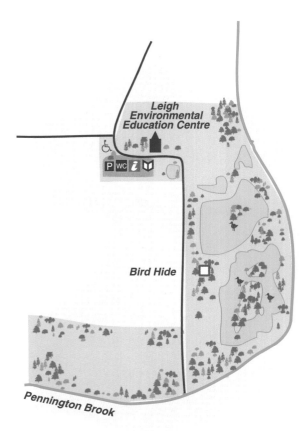

Leigh Environmental Education Centre

Bird Hide

Pennington Brook

HOPE CARR / LEIGH

START & FINISH
Leigh Environmental Education Centre

MAP
O/S Landranger 109 (Manchester)

SURFACE
Gravel/grass

RATING
Easy

PROVISION FOR PEOPLE WITH DISABILITIES
Path suitable for wheelchairs

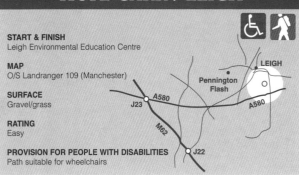

Leigh Environmental Education Centre is situated east of the M6 and Pennington Flash, north of the A580 and Warrington and south of Leigh.

The Centre is a restored 100 year old barn situated within the Hope Carr Nature Reserve. The barn consists of classrooms for children to study the environment. (Please note this facility is available to schools, free of charge) The Hope Carr Nature Reserve covers approximately 37 acres and is open to the public throughout the year. There is also an art and craft centre on site open most days.

A bird hide has been built on the highest point which gives the observer excellent views of the whole site.

The wetland has been developed to provide a variety of habitats for wildfowl and pond life.

North West Water
Community partnerships

EQUIPMENT NOTE: Trainers and sturdy shoes are adequate and it is advisable to take waterproof clothing.

NORTH WEST WATER INFORMATION PUBLICATIONS

North West Water produces a wide range of publications which provide information about our services. To request a copy, simply send your name, address and details of the publications you require to:

North West Water Limited (Dept LR)
1050 Europa Boulevard,
Warrington WA55 1LR

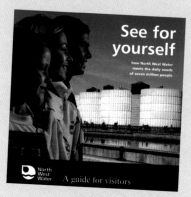

SEE FOR YOURSELF
- Sites to visit
- Education centres
- Recreational sites
- Mobile visitors centres

EXTRA CARE
- Billing Queries
- Home visits
- Passwords
- Braille and large print

A GUIDE TO SAVING WATER
- Your water audit
- In the kitchen
- In the bathroom
- In the garden

PAYING YOUR BILL
- Working it out
- Easy ways to pay
- Where your money goes
- Moving Home

THE WATER BUSINESS
- The water cycle
- Our investment programme
- Working in the community
- Customer service

COMMUNITY COMMITMENTS
- Education
- Environment
- Enterprise Skills
- Regional Leadership
- Extra needs

TO: **PETA EDWARDS**
        Age Concern in the North West
        29 Lunedale Avenue
        Blackpool
        Lancashire FY1 6LL

FROM: Name: ....

        Address: ....

        ....

        ....

        Tel. No. : ....

❑ I would like information on Age Concern's Services

❑ I would like information on becoming a Volunteer for Age Concern

❑ I would like information on Age Concern's range of insurance products

❑ I enclose a donation of   £.............. to Age Concern

All Age Concern organisations in the North West are registered charities

Age Concern Organisations aim to promote the
well-being of all older people and help make later life a
fulfilling and enjoyable experience.

OTHER WILDE'S GUIDES

Wildes cycle Guides show a selection of the very best almost traffic free routes.
These routes are provided in four books covering.

[1] Derbyshire and Cheshire
[2] Lancashire and the Lakes
[3] Yorkshire Dales, Humberside,
     North and West Yorkshire.
[4] Devon, Cornwall and West Somerset.

These are not mountain rides but enjoyable
journeys for the whole family to take at whatever
pace and time they wish. Each route has its own map showing everything you need to know from
distances and directions to parking, picnic and rest stops.

Wildes Cycle Guides are available through bookshops, WH Smiths and selected cycle shops or by
mail order from Gildersleve Publishing. (see address below)

- -

Please send me ☐ 19 trails in Lancs and the Lakes **£6.75**   ☐ 34 trails in Yorkshire and Humberside **£7.50**

☐ 32 trails in Derbyshire and Cheshire **£7.95**   ☐ 30 trails in Devon and Cornwall **£7.95**
New Edition

Name: -

Address: -

- **Postcode:** -

Payment: Credit card ☐   Cheque* ☐   Postal order ☐

20% OFF when you buy 2 or more guides

Credit Card ☐☐☐☐☐☐☐☐☐☐☐☐☐☐☐☐   **Expiry Date** ☐☐☐☐   **Signature** - - - - - - - - - -

*Please make cheques payable to **Gildersleve Publishing Ltd.** Post Payment to:
Gildersleve Publishing Ltd, Capricorn House, Rising Bridge, Lancashire BB5 2AA.

ROUTE NOTES:

North
West
Water

Community
partnerships

51